Poetry in Exile

By Yasin Aziz

Table of Contents

1

Preface

Exile, for me, has a different definition to one who is barred from one's native country; it's when one is isolated from his own loved ones, his community for various reasons, can be poverty, disability, is a child when they cannot be considered or listened to, or being a woman suffering from sexual abuse, parochial and culture repression. But it is also an asylum seeker or a refugee who can be vulnerable to some or all of the above mentioned.

This book is based on my experience of being in exile when I lost my mother when I was eight years old. Ever since, I had to grow up quickly, try to understand my repressive environment and take on life by myself.

Introduction

I had been thinking about writing a book that used poetry, prose and art that tackled the subject of living in exile to write about its effects, impact and consequences, long before I finally put pen to paper.

Through experience, I have found out that one cannot possibly see what the future holds. We often think or fantasise about our hopes and ambitions, especially when we are young. But often, it turns out differently, as it might be expected, for better or for worse. But one thing I am sure about is that it's one's innate ability that makes one try to survive at whatever cost. This survival instinct might be positive in most cases because if one gives in to adversity in life, one may end up with mental or physical illness or death. And that's the main hidden fear for seeking survival and trying to have a good life.

In my early years, I did a lot of different manual jobs; I reached a certain level of education to have some kind of qualification to get an office job. I thought I had a good job managing a farm in an agriculture project with about thirty workers and many pieces of machinery. I was young and ambitious as, in 1981; my management of a sugar beet and wheat farm was one of the best in quality and quantity in Iraq. I think being the best, even only once in early life, set me up to try my best and survive many or most, of the problems I have come across in life. I learned enough English many years before I left to be able to communicate. When I lived in four countries, it took me three years to settle in a country, and finally, in the UK. As I was trying to seek asylum, it happened once that I was imprisoned in solitary confinement in Stockholm, Sweden, and accused of being a terrorist with a group of friends

3

when we sought asylum in February 1983 because we travelled from Tripoli, Libya. I will cover that story a bit later.

When I was young, I loved singing and loved to learn to play the violin, but for cultural and environmental reasons, it was not possible.

How do I relate being in exile to poetry, prose and art? I think that it is the best way to say it is unsayable, as all forms of art come from close expressions, and it's the best way to attract attention from all walks of life.

I think I led a life of persecution from my childhood when I lost my mother at eight years old, and my father was not good enough or not literate enough to look after his family, as I started work very early—I was about ten years old. Therefore, I missed my childhood.

I was born into a culture where one is alone and socially stateless, or may not fit in well enough to be respected in society, and realise you are not respected and being nothing to many around you. It was like that for many, unless you were tugged with the day's required label, from a religious family, who were mostly corrupt and thieves, a politician with a strong tribe who have guns, or mercenaries of any kind who are corrupt and unlawfully rich.

Imagine a child grows up and sees all that and cannot express his opinion. For a society that deprives its own loved ones and women of the right to self-expression, what is there for a child and a woman to hope for in their future life? The child of this kind of society is a refugee in his\her own land and his/her own home. At an early age, a child is not aware of his/her way of life or political symbiosis. It's likely an adult from that sort of society (and without an education) will become ready-made corrupt.

I remember from an early age, I looked around and saw differences and unfairness in the name of religion and patriotism and politics of social, economic, and political life. I thought, 'No, I cannot live like my father and read prayers from a holy book without understanding a word of it. I have to check and understand then decide whether it is right for me or not.'

I think in life, one day, an opportunity may arise if one is smart enough to grab it and take his chance. That's what I did. To get to somewhere where you can freely get what you like to read and learn about life and the world, to have space to do whatever you like to do.

In many cases, war is a chance for change, to try to do something different or change your entire life. Sometimes, things that happen might be dangerous, difficult and distressing at the beginning, but they may create some great opportunities to change your life for the better.

When I left, I knew it was dangerous, difficult and stressful, but the choice of saving my own skin was above everything else. It was exile from country, culture, and way of life. To live perhaps in an alien in what could seem like an alien environment, when everything is different, and when you are different to everyone else. No one considered leaving until the necessity to do so grabbed one by the scruff of the neck, as leaving was followed by many changes one had to make to adapt to a different environment. For me, it was either step onto the battlefield and endure certain death or walk towards the unknown in exile.

Into Exile

In the early 1960s, I lost my mother. That was the first step towards being in exile, as I realised later; I was deprived of her care and love, as no one else could ever replace her. I have missed her ever since. Although I was too young to understand her enormous love and care, as she took me everywhere, often sang for me, and I did so for her whenever she asked me.

I lost my father in the 1974 Halabja bombing during the restart of the Kurdish revolution, when four Iraqi warplanes bombed the towns of Qaladzie and Halabja in the space of four days in April 1974. At the time, I was in the army, doing my compulsory army service. I didn't know what had happened. I had just finished my technical college of agriculture, and did not intend to join the revolution and had to do my army service in order to get a job, hoping for a peaceful life. I joined the Iraqi army to do my compulsory army duty, as everyone had to for about eighteen months to two years, from the age of eighteen or above. It was a strange situation: many young Kurds were deserting the army, but I joined a group of my college friends. It was just a few months before the restart of the Kurdish revolution. We were supposed to have been doing a patriotic duty of our Iraqi compulsory army service; on the day of travelling to the town of Diwanyia, South Iraq, we were taken in lorries like a herd of cattle in January 1974, all the way to the army barrack, It was a nonstop journey, all the way from Slemani to Diwanyia for about 500 miles, with no food or drink. We never thought of it as a patriotic duty, but we had no choice, as our jobs and all our daily living depended on this army service; therefore, everyone had to do it. I had to do it because my father was killed in the town of Halabja, forty miles away from the city, and to help my family. We lost everything and had to move to the city. It was the beginning of a strange journey. In January 1974, we were in the back of a lorry all day and night in the freezing cold weather, for in January, Iraq becomes cold. We huddled together like a family to warm each other up and tried to sleep, but there was hardly any chance because of the hard floor in the back of a lorry and the bumpy road. When we arrived at the army barrack after fourteen hours, it was midnight, and we were exhausted, thirsty and hungry.

When the day broke, we saw army officials come to talk to us and tell us about getting boots and uniforms and the process of training and the timetable of the army barrack. There was another group who were there before us, being trained on wireless communications and Morse code. They were often in the open air and in the sunshine in front of the army barrack building, and we watched them being trained on the use of wireless communications, learning the sound of Morse code: *tee tit tat, tit tit, ta ta tit tit*, etc. I was happy to learn that, but we had to do infantry training first. When the time came for our turn to start learning wireless communication, the revolution restarted after a four-year ceasefire when the government and the revolutionaries would not sign an agreement, so we were not allowed to learn wireless communication on Morse Code management because we were Kurdish, as they thought we would abandon the army and join the revolution.

There were three meals a day: lentil soup and bread in the morning; rice, vegetable, and meat at lunchtime; and similar food in the evening.

After about two months, we were given a week off to visit our families. As we arrived, there were talks about the restart of the war. People were all worried as we had been enduring this revolution / war since 1961, and our generation had grown up with it. People were tired of war, but on the 11th of March 1970, the ceasefire lasted for about four years. That revitalised hopes and ambitions; people longed for peace, but they were pessimistic, as negotiations were not going well.

For the week's holiday, I was back home. I said goodbye to my father, and it was for the last time I saw him. It was early in the morning. I went with my younger brother minutes before I left, passing by the mosque where he was. I sent my brother to call him to say goodbye as if I predicted what would happen in the near future. He was killed along with sixty-two people in the bombing of Halabja on the 26th of April 1974, with TNT bombs when I was back in the army and had no idea what happened at the time.

The Bombing of Halabja, 26th of April, 1974

It was an example of the crimes against humanity, the crimes of genocide committed by the Iraqi Ba'athist regime when it deliberately bombed Kurdish civilians twice within three days. Four French-made Iraqi Sukhoi jets came to bomb Halabja in the mid-afternoon of the 26th of April. People were already expecting them because they had bombed the town of Qaladzyia, one hundred miles away, on the 24th of April and killed over one-hundred and eighty civilians. Many had fled Halabja when they heard this news, but others stayed behind, including young volunteers who wanted to assist in self-defence and to help with casualties. These volunteers dug holes in the ground and prepared bomb shelters. One of the biggest bombs hit the middle of the bazaar, creating a three by four-metre hole which burst the town's main water pipe. All the surrounding shops collapsed and caught fire, and many shopkeepers and passers-by were killed or mutilated.

My brother Taha witnessed the bombing, and this is his story:

'I went to the sweetshop with a banknote to get some change. I looked out and saw my father across the street, standing in front of his shop. A few minutes later, I heard the siren when I was about a hundred yards north of where the TNT bomb dropped in the town centre. I was desperate to find shelter and went into a small shop where I hid under a metal table. A huge explosion shook everywhere so violently that the shop's aluminium shutters shattered, and pieces of metal flew about the place. The metal table saved me. Many other shops were closed, and their shutters were hurled out as if they were all open. A few minutes after the bombing I came out into the street and saw that peshmarga fighters were there helping the victims. I saw two of my cousins nearby. I was very worried about my family, and so I hurried home to find out if they were all right. Then I started looking for my father. On my way, I saw that many doors and windows of shops and houses had been thrown wide open by the explosion. I saw a young man's body. His back was badly wounded, and the flow of blood from his wounds was subsiding. He was one of my friends. It was the first time I had seen the town in such a horrific state.

'There was such a terrifying silence. I started shouting at the top of my voice, desperate to hear someone. No one from among my relatives, family and neighbours replied, and still, I was desperately shouting like mad. People were so shocked that no one would utter a word. I headed towards the mosque with an unconscious willingness in my pace as if I was leaping forward with desperate steps, looking for my father. I met one of my neighbour's sons.

"No, I haven't seen him", the young man said.

'I turned and ran towards my father's shop. I looked at the sweetshop where I had gone to get some change minutes before the bombing. It had collapsed, and nearby, there was the body of a ten-year-old boy, the son of my father's friend. I felt his body. It was still warm. I checked his pulse for any sign of life, but there was none. He was that family's only son. His father, too, was murdered in the bombing. A young, innocent child was killed because of his race. They did not let him live for more than ten years. At that tender age, he was blown apart by the fascist Ba'athist's bomb. Nearby, there was a big hole from the TNT explosive that had landed in the middle of adjoining streets, causing most of the fire, destruction and death.

'Water from the burst pipe had created a big pond. Survivors were working to put out fires, collect corpses–there were about 20 bodies near the centre of the blast and more elsewhere–and take the injured to the local hospital. My father's shop had been burned to the ground, but there was no sign of him anywhere. "They took several bodies to the mosque," a young man told me.

'They were taking corpses to all the town's mosques, and I went around them, checking the clothes of victims whose bodies were about to be taken to the graveyard. But I did not find my father. I kept going, checking all Halabja's mosques. They were overwhelmed with corpses. When I heard that some bodies had been taken to mosques in Sirwan village, I began that 10-kilometre journey but soon came across my sisters and my brother coming back from the village. They assured me that our father was not there.

'We spent the night with no news of him, and early in the morning, we started looking for him again with a few relatives and friends who came to help us. We searched among the debris of the collapsed shops and buildings but still found no trace of him.

'The next night, we all felt desperate. One of my sisters woke us up early, crying about her dream. "I saw my father", she said. "He told me, 'Come, I am here. You can find me here.'"

"I know where he is", she kept saying. "Wake up, let's go. I know where he is".

'Across the road from father's shop and close to the TNT bomb site, a two-storey building behind the sweetshop had collapsed, and we started lifting its debris. Then we found him. His body was all crushed, flattened almost like a piece of paper. It was such a terrible spectacle. No one would ever wish to see their father like this. It was so horrific. The scene would never leave our memories. This was what Arab Muslim brothers did to Kurds.

'With the help of neighbours, relatives and friends, we moved the debris and collected father's remains. These were not even in the shape of a human body. We collected his remains in a sack and took them to the mosque. The agony of trying to find him had been replaced by the certainty of grief. Our father had had nothing to do with the politics of the revolution. He was about 60 years old and one of sixty-three people killed in the bombing, with more than a hundred injured.'

That was an episode in the life of revolution in Halabja. At the time, almost no one knew that there was much worse to come. The majority naively thought that this was the ultimate grief and distress.

The revolutionaries had trained their anti-air force guns on the four French-made Iraqi fighter jets, especially the gunner on the fourth floor of the 'Tankih, Tobacco' building who kept firing with a submachine gun. But it was obviously not enough to deter the planes from dropping TNT bombs on the civilian population in the high street. This was the centre of the town, where many shops and the bazaar were situated. Targeting a civilian population certainly amounted to the crime of genocide—just like two days before, when they killed 200 civilians, mainly college and university students, in the town of Qaladiza. But the bombing failed to destroy the revolution. Instead, it added more sore wounds to the determination of the revolutionaries, making them fight harder than ever before. By April, the war started, and we in the army were barred from asking for any break, even though we were not allowed to go to Baghdad, as many often would do for the weekend break.

12

We often did tune in to the revolution's radio and were anxious to know what was happening in so-called North Iraq, Kurdistan.

There was news of the war on the frontline in many parts, as the government ordered attacks to recapture the revolutions / Peshmarga area in the Kurdistan Mountains but often were defeated.

Many Kurds were trying to desert the army, but I did not want to. After a while, I learned my family moved to Baghdad as we had relatives there and sent me news not to desert the army.

One weekend, on the 30th of April, I tried to go with a group of friends to go to Baghdad. It was the 1st of May 1974, 'The Workers Day'. I knew my family were in Baghdad, in Bab al-Sheikh and Battaween, and had their phone number. We boarded the Basrah–Baghdad train in Nasryia train station, were happy to have a weekend break, and some were thinking about making fake holiday permission papers to go back home, or desert the army, as I was offered to do so, but did not want to. As close friends, we had a lot of trust and friendship; no one would think about spying on others.

After a few hours from the town of Diwaniya, or at Mahmoodyia, a village about half an hour from Baghdad, our carriage train cabins were suddenly blocked from both ends with Enzibat; patrol Soldiers, inspectors with red berets. We were twenty-six soldiers, and all were arrested, were put in army lorries and taken away. We didn't know where, until our lorry entered a big army compound, and got off in a row towards a low roofed building, a deputy army officer sitting on a wood chair, 'Nayeb zabit' a dark slim, sallow-faced deputy officer, sitting on a chair stared at us and aggressively shouting:

'There are two hundred army controls from Baghdad to the North, 'shimal' in Arabic how can you manage to pass through all that? He was mockingly sneering at us.' Obviously, we could say nothing. Even if we did, they would not believe us. We were all taken to a room without further

13

interviews or investigations. It was in the evening, and the army compound was al Harithyia army barrack, with its known notorious prison. We were all asked to go into that room. It was about 6x6 metres, with a bucket for peeing and defecating, and nothing else, no water, no food. We were all worried about our fate if we might end up in the known Baathist jail, the Palace of the End, 'Qasri nihayia' as anyone taken there, would never come out. It was an evening I will never forget; they kept bringing prisoners, of all types, drunk, mad, sad. We could never ask, or we were not sure if we should ask why they were brought in, as we thought our lives were in the balance.

They brought about seventy that evening, hardly any space to sit. We could never lie down or sleep or get comfortable. I saw many lying down, crisscrossing each other's bodies as they were trying to sleep. It was a fearful and strange evening; any clinging of metal or jingling of the keys would alert us to check whether they were coming for us. There was no thought of food, drink or proper sleep, as we did not know what was going to happen to us.

In the morning, we heard the door and clinging metals and keys, and I heard one of our friends tell the one next to him a few lines of a lyric:

'Shirin, 'sweetheart'

'Shirin it's spring, the season of happiness,
Not for the deprived, and the unfulfilled dreams.
Do not shiver with fear from hearing the clinging chains;
They are for the flesh and not for the determined to live'.

That was a revolutionary poem by one of our Kurdish poets.

Soon, a few soldiers with their sergeant called our names and handcuffed us in twos. I was handcuffed with a friend I used to know from around my town. We sort of smiled, as we looked like chained young calves. We all were taken by army tracks to the train station, and they let us buy egg and tomato sandwiches with salad. It was so delicious; we were starving, as we did not have any food or water for the last twenty-four hours, and we were accompanied by Arab soldiers, Enzibats, and patrol soldiers on a train carriage back to our army barracks. We were pleased to be back at the army barracks, as if we were home in Kurdistan.

When we arrived back, we were sent to the barrack's prison. The day after, a senior officer of the army division called us individually for investigation, for each of us to explain his case. The group with me from the same barrack were sentenced to five days imprisonment; it was a relief to get away so lightly. As soon as we were released, we were sent away. They didn't let us see each other; rather, we were scattered to different places in various army barracks in South Iraq.

I was sent to Nasiriya Territorial Army across the Euphrates River from the city. I ended up with a small group of Kurds and Arabs in the army fire brigade, with a deputy army officer in charge, trained as an army fire brigade soldier.

Our barrack was a hut-like hall with metal springy beds, each separated about two or three yards from each other'. It was fine compared with others' army duties and conditions as we had not much to do early in the morning, and after inspection, with some walking and running exercise, we were all on duties with an axe in a leather folder and standing by the telephone waiting in turns on guard for a fire call up if there was any fire to put out.

One night we were called to a village on fire, far away from the city. By the time we arrived with our fire engine, the village was almost burned down. There were no human casualties, but a few cattle and calves had been burned alive.

On another occasion, we were called from the Ur desert army barrack to the west of the city as an army compound, and ammunition bunks were on fire. We were lucky it took us over an hour to reach, as, by the time we arrived, all the ammunition had exploded.

My time at the fire brigade division was fine; we were not under any pressure, as Kurds often faced racial harassment and abuse concerning the situation in Kurdistan. The ones who stayed in the Iraqi army wanted to finish the army service and find employment to help their family, as in every war and revolution, not everyone is at war.

I finished my army service in March 1976. I was pleased to have managed to complete my army service without getting in any trouble or facing pressure to desert the army. I was back in my city to try to find employment in the agricultural section of the Kurdish area near my city. Although I possessed sufficient qualifications from the technical college of Agriculture of the Bakrajow village near the city, I had to try had gain employment where it was convenient and where I wanted.

When I found a job, I was young. I had a few projects before me, and I was sort of excited thinking about when to get married, but I did not know my coming years would be totally different from what I was looking forward to. It did not take long until I was called again, this time as an army reservist, to do six months of army service. I had to go to the same city as Nasiriya. I had no choice. I had to, for if I did not go to do that, I would lose my employment. But this time, the army service was bad and very difficult, as I was not sent to the fire brigade that I was qualified for in my first army service. I was sent to the territorial headquarter of the Nasiriya army compound. I had to do manual labour work during the day, and guard the army headquarter of Division 1, 'Failaq 1' at night. It was very harsh. I did not like that at all. I felt as if we were used like slaves.

The rule was to do as you were told. If not, you would be imprisoned and raped in prison. I swore I wouldn't do another army service when I finished my service. As I was released after six months, I returned to my office work at the agricultural department, Slemani Sugar factory. It was about a year later I decided to go on holiday abroad for the first time. I took a month's leave in August 1980 and went to Bulgaria via Turkey on a nearly forty-hour coach journey.

I was about twenty-six years old. I went on holiday with a friend who was a teacher. I got to know him through my other friends. When anyone travelled, they had to get permission from the government, apart from taking leave from my office job. It took a while to get the papers and passport ready. I borrowed 300 Iraqi Dinar from my office finance department to pay back in instalments, which was worth about $1,000, and it was more than enough for the return coach tickets and all other expenses for a month's holiday.

We paused on the way a few times but sitting for so long made our guts stiff. We would not be able to eat, as whatever we had eaten in the last hours was still there waiting to be released, but our intestines were hardened like a rock. When we arrived in Istanbul, it took a long time to discharge our inside loads. We stayed the night in Istanbul.

The day after, we had booked with another company to go to Varna in Bulgaria; oh, it was a paradise, so colourful, beautiful, green, and cool. As the time we left home, it was August, very dry and hot. But Varna revitalised our stifled energy, spirit and ambitions. It was a life-changing trip.

Sometimes, there were spits of rain here and there on sunny days. The black sea side was crowded with people, and one could see as far as one looked, so many were having a nice time on the golden sand. One side was blue, and the other was green, and in between was a stretch of pale golden sand.

With the money we had, we could exchange one hundred dollars for three hundred Levs the then Bulgarian currency. Our holiday was for a month; about a week on the way, coming and going. We stayed one night each way in Istanbul and the rest in Varna and Sofia, mostly Varna. Although Sofia was beautiful and clean, Varna was the right place for a holiday and for leisure.

We went back, vitalised and full of stories of boasting about the holiday, and I thought, 'Yes, I will never do Iraqi army service anymore'. Iraq was not my 'watan' (country, as Arabs say). As the army service showed us, we were slaves, not compatriots. We Kurds have never had a fair share of human respect and resources, as the Arabic language was the official language, and we were deprived of all our basic human rights.

The trip to Bulgaria was an eye opener; even at the time I was on holiday, there were Kurds in exile from the previous Kurdish revolution, as the superpowers' one centre of business resources.

As I came back to Iraq at the end of August, on September 18th, the Iraq/Iran war began about ten days later, so it was obvious I would be called again to go to the army, specifically to go to war, when the war had nothing to do with me or us Kurdish people. It was crazy to go to war for an Arab regime that did not treat us like a normal human beings.

Not only did I not go, but I managed to put many off going to do that slavish army service and get killed for the fascist ethos of pan–Arab nationalism.

After the war had raged for about a year and a half, I was called to the army, but I had done my own preparation to leave before I was called. A month before I left, I went to the area where I had to plan. This was the way of leaving, by going into exile through the chain of Border Mountains between Iraq and Iran. It was exactly the battlefield area between the two sides at war.

Often through my childhood, I was mesmerised by the thought of when I could explore this high and Rocky Mountains over 5,000 metres high.

I set out with a friend from my town, Halabja, who waited in the Shiramar village at the feet of Surein Mountain towering over the Sharazur Plain, situated 'between the town of Halabja and the city of Slemani', in the Sharazur plain. We stayed with a family who were my mother's cousins for two nights waiting for a group of Kurdish Peshamrga to come down, as they often did and stayed in the village to replenish. On the second day, there were about twenty-four peshmarga gunmen in the village. We had to climb the rugged mountain terrain, an area of the battle between the Iraqi army and the so-called Islamic Republic of Iran in 1982.

We stayed for a few days at the Surein Mountain base, called Gulakhana village, or ex village, as it was destroyed by Saddam's forced relocation campaign of 5,000 Kurdish villages, at the hilly foot of the Surein Mountain, with its towering enormity and defiance, overlooking the Iraqi army barracks of the Sharazur plain.

19

It was the 12th of June, 1982

One dark early morning at 3:30 am, we woke up and got ready to leave the mountain base. A few peshmarga hurriedly made salty fried bread.

The terrain felt like pieces of copper and iron flakes that clashed and cluttered under our feet as we stepped forward, blindly accompanied by the dark heaps of the mountains on our left. We were heading towards the peaks of the Dzli Mountain, towards the Iranian border check further north.

When the day broke, we were above the Khurmal town, bare and treeless. Below and opposite were the town's army barracks. We had to hurry up because the Iraqi soldiers could easily shoot us all within a few minutes.

I saw my friend stopping to adjust the zip of his shoulder bag and said, 'Look, that is the army barracks facing us with their tanks and heavy submachine guns. What are you doing? Hurry up, let's go!'

At the time, this trip was supposed to be for a few years 'until the war finished.' It never crossed my mind that I would spend most of my life in exile and that exile would become my destiny and way of life.

For about eight hours, the twenty-six men went up and down. About halfway, a few hours before reaching the summit of the 9,000-foot mountain, there was a narrow path bending around an enormous peak. On the way, we would have to pass an Iraqi army post on the hillside to the right. They gathered to discuss tactics. Someone in the group, a senior peshmarga, said, 'This is the most dangerous part of our trip to reach the border crossing and the summit; the crossing line between Iraq and Iran'. Round the bend from where we sat, there was an Iraqi army post overlooking the narrow path. The path was only about thirty yards away from the Iraqi army post. The Iraqi army could shoot us all, but there was no alternative. 'Oh God, this is it, either we make it or we will be killed', I thought.

The senior Peshmerga seemed to be anxious as he suggested that the two unarmed men should go first. My friend looked at each other and said nothing. We had no choice but to either pass that dangerous spot or go back home. We could not say 'No' since, in the culture, no man should look scared. Soon someone else shouted, 'No, No! Those two are unarmed and should not go first. Another two who are armed should go'. It was a slight relief, even though the danger was not over yet.

Two Peshmarga went around the bend. There was no sound of shooting. Then it was the turn of my friend and me. We set off with our shoulder bags slung to the right and tried to walk as normally as possible. We walked past the army post, and thankfully, no soldier saw us and pulled his trigger. In the space of a few minutes, I passed the most dangerous test of my life.

We reached safety and anxiously waited until everyone else had completed the ordeal. No one was shot. Then we went down to a rocky valley and sat around a water spring and ate some fried bread.

On our way through this rocky valley called Mlakhurd, it looked as though, on both sides of the mountain path, there were two rocky walls going up high until they kissed the pale blue morning sky.

Thinking we had passed danger from the Iraqi side, we spread out leisurely. Most of the gunmen shot at shrubs, trees and rocks as though they were testing their prowess and showing off. One of the gunmen, Omar, was from the nearby Khurmal town and was a friend of my cousin. Omar gave me his Kalashnikov and said, 'You can have a go too'. It was as though Omar didn't want me to feel left out. I shot a shrub on a rocky, but U didn't really care if I hit the target, and nor did Omar.

For hours, we were climbing up and up, with no end in sight. It felt and looked as if so many mountains were thrust one on top of the other. I kept looking up, hoping this would be the last.

'No brother, you should not look up. There are many more we have to climb,' Omar kindly told me.

Someone called out from behind them, 'No one should eat Ballaluk, that sweet berry'. He warned everyone because the berry caused dehydration, and there would be no water spring until we reached the summit.

Ballaluk is a grown wild shrub in summer with fruits like tender soft colourful beads, yellow, orange, red, orange, and black. It has a bitter-sweet taste and is grown between mountain rocks.

When we nearly reached the summit, Iranian troops tried to ambush them. The Iranians fired some shots, but the Peshmerga managed to persuade them that they were supposedly their Kurdish friends, not Iraqi foes. As we were about to reach the summit at 11.20 am, I turned to my right to see my town, Halabja, which seemed covered in a hazy yellowish dust. We were so exhausted and thirsty. We all lay down under the shade of weeping willows and drank from a cool, sweet mountain water spring. I turned to my left and, on a green peak, despite the everyday bombings, shootings and killings a little partridge was carelessly singing... *qakie ba qakie ba qakie ba... qak.* It looked so content and happy with the green and refreshing breeze.

At the summit, we met Iranian republican guards who checked our passports and papers. The guards sent us to another group of gunmen on the Iranian side of the border who gave us some bread and watermelon and then in the back of a Toyota pickup car, to the little town of Merivan on the other side of the Surein mountain.

The Toyota pickup sped up on the dusty road, drove off, and for the first time, we were lost in the fog of the thick dust of lost dignity and pride, and then the life of asylum seekers in exile began...

Ten years later, when I was in London, in my white city flat at W12 7LY, I wrote the following poem, the Little Partridge:

22

The Little Partridge

I was climbing the mountains, when you were on the green summit,
I was drenched with sweating in mid-June heat, when I saw you
And heard you singing, I confess, I felt a sense of defeat.
As I was leaving, you were still there, I felt wretched, miserable, sad
You didn't care.
Oh, the little partridge, at the time, I didn't make out your sweet song. I
didn't know leaving the country and you would last so long.
It is now 10 years since; it took me so
Long to understand your warning message.

When we arrived at the town of Marivan, a small town on the other side of the border of the Surein Mountain, my friend contacted Iranian security service. We said, 'We were army deserters did not want to fight for Saddam's regime and have come to go abroad'.

We were sent to the Red Crescent centre and stayed for three days, then we were sent to the Kurdish city of Sanandaj in the city I had a family relative, who were relatives of my father, I had their name, when we were staying at the Red Crescent centre of Sanandaj, I found a chance to leave, as we were not allowed, as they said, 'for our safety'.

Where we were staying was close to the city centre. As we found a chance with a friend I met on the way when we were leaving for exile, we jumped over the locked door, I mean 'illegally left the office,' went to find the family, as I knew the family name.

As we were staying close to the city centre, I saw a busy indoor market in the lower ground of the bazar, it seemed like an old-style building with many vaults built with red bricks, with shops built into the walls and over a metre-high bench in front of the shops. I looked around, and I found an old man sitting on the brick bench before his shop. I saluted him and asked for the family I was looking for and gave the family name, as I thought the family must be well-known and easily recognised because they were native to the city. The man knew them and gave me an easy way to find them as they had a shop nearby. He said, 'Yes I know them. If you go out back from where you came in, as you leave the gate, climb and cross over, as you go up, you'll see another market opposite in the lower ground, you can see the second shop on the right is their shop'.

There was a young man about fifteen or sixteen. I told him I was a family relation from Kurdistan of Iraq, and 'I would like to see your family, to let them know I am here and going abroad soon'.

He asked where I was staying. I gave him the name and address of the place.

'Oh, that is just a few minutes walking from our house.'

We decided in the evening I would be going there, as I did not know when we were leaving the Red Crescent office to go to Tehran, not to miss out on meeting them. It was a strange meeting, as we lived in two different countries. We needed a passport and visa to see each other, but it was our country that was divided by victors of the First World War, as they divided the area as they wished.

The lady who was the mother of the boy I met in the shop welcomed me and asked about my family and all the relatives. Her younger son was so pleased to meet me. They did not let me go back to the centre that evening, so I slept there. Before we went to bed, the younger boy brought the family photo album and showed me all the family and their relatives that I never knew anything about. It was such a strange co-incident amongst all the photos. I found my mother's photos. I recognised her. I was so pleased because my mother died when I was young and I never had a photo of her, as I remembered after her death we could not find any, as we were grown up and needed to see what she looked like, or my younger brothers and sisters never remembered what she looked like, but for me, I was delighted, as I missed her so much. I gave it to a friend, who was a family relation, to make a few copies and sent them to my family.

A few years later, when I was in London, UK, and after I did my GCSEs and was doing my A-Level in English, I wrote the following:

My Mum and the Mountains

I was only eight when my mum passed away
It was so strange, I was too young
To ask why,' what is the reason, she's just gone'
How come, she never told me, had nothing to say?
Ever since she's never been back
Whenever I heard others call their sons
And they said, 'Yes, mum?'
I remembered your singing tunes, when
I used to squat near you plying dough
With your soft fingers, making bread
The thin layer turned rosy, swelled and
For me you sung.
It took me so long to understand
How you cared for me, but why
so soon you left, why in a hurry
to heaven?
Many years have passed, I just realized
When after a few days mourning,
my first visit to the cemetery, as everyone
Wanted to leave, I didn't want to go home
I lied down next to your grave
That is where I wanted to stay.
Oh, mum at the time I was too young
To understand what was really going on.
I was left with such a huge emptiness for so long.
I remember, in spring we used to go
To the mountains, green beautiful plains
To pick herbs and flowers in the spring days' long hours
Until you suddenly said, 'let's go home, it's getting dark too late.'
I wish I could tell you a bit more now about
Beautiful days together so happily we passed.
The days of picnic in the mountains, orchards and ravines,
for launch, and exploring so many beautiful scenes.
I wish you could hear me now telling you about

All these, or at least once more to see your
Innocent smiles of motherly care and just
A few more melodies, tunes…

Two days after that visit, we went to Tehran, the capital of Iran. We stayed for a few days in a refugee camp called Parki Eiram'. It was said it used to be one of the previous kings of Iran's parks, and turned into a refugee camp with trees and green spaces all around.

We stayed for a few days, and then, when I heard there was another detention centre further out of Tehran and some army deserters like us were staying there because a few of them were my relatives and friends, I asked to go there.

It was Ramadan, the Muslim fast when people don't eat and drink from dawn to dusk for a month, but we were over that ethos. We never fasted. The place was called Karaj Park, a town a few miles outside of Tehran. The place consisted of a few big halls with rows of single metal beds, with a few blankets each. We were given meals in the evening, and long before the day break, I did not eat and kept it for later in the morning, but my friend ate it and later asked me to share mine. I refused and said, 'Why you ate with the ones who fast, but you don't fast? You should keep it for later like me.

We were allowed to go to Tehran to take a bath. As there were no showers or baths in the camp but in the city, we could not eat during the day. We bought food and ate it in the public bath's private rooms, as in the bath we had our own private rooms.

After about seven weeks in Iran, we had to bribe the corrupt officials to process our departure papers for Bulgaria with a tourist visa. In Bulgaria, there was still the same anxiety about where to go next, every night, going to bed without knowing what the next day would bring to the direction of our asylum, seeking a path and our destiny.

At Sofia airport, the communist police treated us badly: we were ushered aside to be checked like a herd of sheep or cattle. We all had some money to pay for the flight and expenses. We tried hard to hide them, as we thought the police would take them from us, and then we could do nothing about it after a while. Later, I heard the checking became more severe or thorough, as one of my friends had his shoe sole torn off by the Bulgarian airport police.

As the police would not believe us if we had no money on us, the airport became like an ambush for victims of war to be robbed of their money and properties.

We became so many, as more army deserters arrived, some with families and others single; the airport did not let us depart to where we wanted to go—Europe—so we were stuck, running out of money. Some had more money and could bribe the airport police in Sofia to let them.

The Iraqi embassy and the UN knew about us. They came to where we were staying. I never wanted to meet any of them myself, for I did not want to go back to become the fuel of Saddam's wars.

When the Bulgarian UN branch learned about our situation, we were running out of money and could not leave the country. They found somewhere for us, a holiday camp called Cherenkov on the periphery of the Bulgarian capital. It was a beautiful place next to the Vitosha or Vitoza mountain, with plenty of orchard trees and shrubs. It had a sort of mountainous landscape with porta cabins or small flats made of wood. It was like a camping site or a holiday resort. There were other tourists staying; it was nearly the end of the summer holiday season in 1982.

We, the singles, took part in some parties in the evening. There was music and dancing with other tourists as if trying to escape from the dilemma, anxiety, and uncertainty of our daily life in Sofia, as we stayed for nearly two months.

I picked up some Bulgarian and bought a handbook for learning the language. We were there for seven weeks, and by the time I left, I was able to communicate with Bulgarian people, and was often asked, 'Are you a student?'

I said, 'No, I have just been here for about two months'.

We became a group of forty, a few families including nine single men, as we all tried to leave Iraq and escape the war. One of our young men contacted the Libyan embassy in Sofia, the capital of Bulgaria. And we were told, 'Yes, we can all go and work there, it is your country, there is no need for refugee status, you can work and make some money like a million and a half foreigners live there.'

I ran out of money. A family from my town was with us and lent me the price of the flight to Tripoli. We boarded the plane and arrived at about 3:30 hours. It was about midnight when we arrived in Tripoli.

We stayed for over an hour and a half until a few Mercedes buses came to take us. We were not told where we were going, and we ended up in a hotel called Hotel Shatee, a hotel overlooking the Mediterranean Sea. We were given rooms for singles, two people in one room, and the families were given a room or two each according to how many persons each family consisted of. One of us called his friend, 'Look, it is desert and camel again, oh God, we ended up somewhere similar to South Iraq.' Many of us intended to go to Sweden.

The morning after, we woke up with dazzling hot sunshine and the glow of the glittering sea. It hurt our eyesight, as we were not used to it.

A group of us came down dressed up, waiting for the government officials to come and welcome us. For a few days, no one came, 'it seemed strange for the Arab tradition to treat us like that, not being respected, as they promised in Sofia. It showed the first signs of being stateless.

A few of us had suits, got dressed up and waited a few mornings. After a few days, they gave up, as they realised no one would come, or not yet, as if they were not interested or, for whatever reason, reluctant to see us. We had accommodation and food, but that was not the reason we left our country.

We sometimes tried to swim as an attempt to fill up some parts of our free time, as we had nothing to do. A few of us could swim well, but the rest were trying in the shallow water.

In the first few days, I tried with one or two friends to go to the city centre; wherever we went, it was deserted as if most of the people were detained at home for some reason. There were no cafes, bars or good restaurants, or anything to attract one's attention for passing some time, and that beautiful seaside was full of boredom. It was a pity for the Mediterranean seaside to be seen so dead-silent and lonely.

It seemed there was always some fine dusty wind or some traces of it. The yellowish-brown desert dust took refuge at the groves and slits of the kerbs and potholes along the pavements that were matched by the pale and light yellow colour of the surrounding concrete buildings. There were hardly any shops open, and it took us a while to find out, all the retail and food shops were in multi-story shopping centres, but the people seemed to be content. They had nice houses in white, light yellow, light grey or beige, and many had cars, jobs, and plenty of money, yet far away from the aggressive claws of modern capitalism.

The Gadhafi government had a sort of dictatorial socialist system, but people had jobs, cars, houses, and peace. The peace was so precious, as we left everything we loved because of war. The Libyans seemed content.

Whatever was said in the media about Gadhafi's dictatorial regime during his downfall, to be fair, was both misinformation and disinformation. The culture was tribal, and the conversation was rowdy or comparable to loud shootings; they wore cream or white tunic, a sort of similar colour overall and a 'fez' (a North African hat) or a turban. The women were well wrapped and, apart from a few with their family, seemed quite liberal. Many of them were beautiful.

After a few months in the hotel: as I was told by my friends that someone had come to see us, or to welcome us. It was better late than never, and we were asked which one of us was the elder of the group to organise a political party as another opposition to Saddam's regime. But we were not interested in collaborating, even though we were offered money, flats and cars, and options to visit Europe with our new political agenda, but we refused; even if one or two of us may have been interested, the majority were not. We stayed playing cards, sitting in the ground floor huge lobby, going to the seaside, about 100 yards far from our rooms. There were many African visitors, some Europeans staying in the hotel.

In the first week, the water we drank tasted bitter or salty. As they said, the hotel had some water/plumbing problems. Even the red orange juice we often had in the restaurant tasted bitter. The summer glittering sea was blindly hurtful to our eyes. As we had no work, we could easily feel all the pros and cons of our unexpected new life on the South Mediterranean shore in North Africa.

As most of us had little to no money left, the thought of exploring the country was not on anyone's mind; it was certain we were not tourists, but what should we have been called? No one knew. All our passports were taken by the immigration officials at Tripoli airport, and we were never told for how long or when we would get them back. It took seven months for some of us to have them returned.

We often met up in the ground floor lobby or in our rooms, or the men met more often, as we had no Libyan friends.

We asked for jobs; we did not want to be fed and accommodated free of charge, but there was no response. It was obvious we were stuck and could do nothing about it, and a few times, we were paid with money, but we wanted jobs, not free money. In our culture, we were not used to it.

As we met so often, we learned about each other's life stories or profiles by heart. After a few months, most of our conversations became repetitive and boring. After a while, we found out there were a few officials from the Kurdish and Iraqi opposition parties in Tripoli. They often came to Libya for money, and some of them were supposedly staying in our hotel. They often came to have a cup of tea or coffee with us and to talk about their political agenda.

A few of us seemed to have considered ourselves to have taken the side of one or other organised group, militia or political party. A few of us often went to see them, to have a coffee or cup of tea with them and talk about how our asylum-seeking group ended up in Libya. I spoke enough English to communicate, so I could narrate the story of our Mediterranean Sea accidental venture, but it was not needed until I met the head of the UN office in Tripoli later.

After about six months, we had no work and no prospect of leaving the country. Half of our group decided to leave for Sweden. Those of us who wanted to leave were given our passports back, and tickets bought for us by the Libyan government via Switzerland Zurich to Stockholm, Sweden.

In Sweden, all the men were separated from their families and put in prison. We ended up in solitary confinement in Stockholm's eight-story police building, in the middle of the city, in police cells. They treated us like criminals without any trial for about two weeks with very little food. I was starving, not allowed to see each other or anyone, and had no access to the press or any lawyers. Stockholm was the capital of human rights in the world —it was awful, inhuman, and barbaric. It was a very small room, with a bed. I often had to walk in that little space of over metres until I got tired, and then I had to lie down. There were cameras in the room, so I knew we were being watched.

They gave us very little food: some green peas, a few little biscuits, a coffee; it was not our food, but we had no choice, for I was starving, lying down dreaming of chicken, rice, bread, and meat, salivating in my sleep, dreams of my childhood war, cries, and the noise of mourning crowds. It was similar to Saddam's prisons, as I had friends tell me about their experience in Iraq's prison. Even when we knocked on the door to go to the toilet or to take a shower, we were not allowed to see each other. After a few days, I started knocking and punching the door like mad. Someone from the police entered in a black suit and white shirt. I asked him, 'Why you are doing this to us? We are not criminals. Prove it if we are! You are so cruel and inhuman'.

He asked me, 'How many millions are you?'

I replied, 'So? What do you mean? We are not all coming here, even if your government let us stay, we will pay tax, we are all ready to work and pay taxes, but you spend tens of thousands for your people to reach adult age to work and pay tax, we are ready made taxpayers'.

He said, 'We will send you all back to Libya'.

I said, 'I won't go. If they are going back, I won't. We all have different cases. I am not coming on holiday or to see your country, I ran away from a war, left my job and all my loved ones'.

33

He left me at that, and after a while, another day, there was an interpreter. As I was called, I said, 'I'm not going back, I don't want to go to war or kill anyone, and l came here seeking peace'. But it seemed I was trying in vain, as the day I was called to be taken away was to the airport. We were sent back in three groups. Our first group were three single men. As soon as they arrived at Tripoli airport, they were detained and were told they would be sent back via Amman, Jordan, to Baghdad. They would face execution by Saddam's regime. Luckily, one of them had the phone number of the Kurdish group left in Tripoli. He phoned a Kurdish family in the hotel and told them what was happening.

The family found some connection and went to one of Gadhafi's men. He was called Dr Muftah. They found him at home and told him what was happening. He phoned the airport, and they let them in, and then, for us, the third group re-entry was clear for the two families and me.

Years later, concerning what happened to us in Sweden, I wrote the following:

I thought

I left the war. I paced along terrains of mines, creeping ambush, often a sudden blow.
 I started on the landscape of darkness, along heaps of monstrous shadows, still stepped along, with creaking flakes of copper, irons in the mountains of the battlefield,
 to search for a right path, the way for peace, so determined, no way, there's no defeat.
I thought 'Yes, I am going, I won't give up whatever happens,
yes I have to leave, no way to hesitate,
 Oh God, what an enormous task, it's just I try to live..."
Yes, no way to give up, I have to carry on, yet going, 'defying unpredictable destiny's blazing grips,

to drench my soul from its long anticipation for a smile of welcome, often with a screwed frown, a twisted face.

'No, no I won't give up hope, as from the day I came to be, I have been trying all venues of life searching for peace.'

I went along during the days of scorching heat, looking for a shelter, a place of refuge, to start again on an unfamiliar path, a new setting, culture, anxious just like I was gasping in the mountains' battlefield, weary of a frowning stare, a sneering grin is just like a bomb with unpredictable outcome, not sure what to do, as I'm on my own.

In my new environment, I was expecting rejection again and again. Yet, I was trying hard to find peace. Once I ended up in solitary confinement for two weeks, starving with hardly any food, no fresh air.

Yes, it's February 1983 in the middle of Stockholm police cell's eight-story building, Sweden, supposedly the heaven of human rights..

I was treated just like a terrorist, not allowed any civilised justice.

It's an experience I will never forget or forgive. Soon after that, certainly, I was rejected and dismissed. Where I was, on the wall, there was a message in Arabic by a Palestinian said, 'I have been in this hell for six months.' Why for some people like us, that's it, the way to live or try to live?

It was a frightening experience to stay there long, especially when one had no criminal offence. That's why I let them send me back. If I had stayed, I wouldn't know for how long before I would go mad or dead from starvation.

'It looked like the same Sweden of about 1415 AD when they invited all nobilities of Denmark for a friendly visit and killed every single one of them' (from the UK Radio 4 programme about Denmark and Sweden historical relations).

It happened once when I was there for about two weeks. One day the guard of my room asked me, 'Do you want to go upstairs to breathe some fresh air?'

I was pleased, and said 'Yes'. When I went in the lift a few stories up to the roof, it was like entering a cage. I was let in, but it was freezing: it must have been about -20 Celsius. I was jumping up and down. I could not stay still for a few seconds, and I had to jump so as not to freeze to death. I could not stay for more than a few minutes and let the police officer know, 'It is enough,' and 'it's too cold'.

After about two weeks, we were sent back via Zurich, Switzerland, to Tripoli, Libya. When we arrived, there was no problem getting in, and I did not know what happened to the rest of the group who were sent back before us or not.

We waited for a while. It must have been over half an hour. There were two families and me; we were taken by a Mercedes bus. It was going towards a different hotel. It was a five-star hotel. We could not believe it. As we entered, one of my friends asked me could you ask the reception if we were booked here. As I asked, the man said yes.

So we were given rooms in a fourteen-story 5-star 'Bab Al Bahr' hotel, the gate of the sea. We could not believe it; it took us a few days to overcome that surprise.

When the rest of the group knew where we were, they were so surprised they came to see us quite often.

'So, to live in exile became the journey of revelations.'

When I was in the star-star hotel, many foreigners and politicians were coming to stay. By then, I had known a few Kurdish politicians. One of them once asked me if I wanted to meet Dr Akram Jaff, from Halabja, my town, who was the head of UNICEF in Rome, Italy. He was in the hotel. I said, 'Yes, of course, I don't mind.'

Then he gave his room number, which was the number of the telephone extension.

I rang his number from my room and told him who I was, then we agreed to meet in the reception area, and later, we met at about 7 pm. I did not even know what he looked like. I saw someone standing by the reception desk. I approached. He spoke in Kurdish. We shook hands and sat for a while. He asked about how we were doing, and I talked about what had happened and did not know whether he could help in anyway, or I did not like to ask if he could help us, then we left it at that.

He was Dr Akram Jaff from where I come from, who had been an ambassador in Africa for some years and then became the head of UNICEF in Rome.

A few days later, at about 11: am, as I was coming down to the lobby, he called me when he was with a few officially dressed European-looking men.

He introduced me to the head of Tripoli UN, Aldo Sisignyano. My English was good enough to explain myself and what we were going through.

He gave his office number and said, 'We will arrange for you to come to my office,' and told me not to talk about our situation if anyone else was around. I knew I was taking a risk, as the Libyan government would not be pleased if I said anything bad about the Libyan government.

One day I went to have a chat with him and explained what happened to us, the Kurdish group in Libya. He tried to arrange a UN passport for us, even filled in forms for all of us, and it was risky if the Libyans knew what I was trying to do. After waiting for a few months, there was no reply.

After seven months of waiting to get a job, we were all sent to Bengasi and were each given a job. I stayed in touch with the head of the UN in Tripoli even after we were sent to Benghazi.

After being in a star-star hotel for a month, and seven months in Tripoli, we were sent to Benghazi on the east side of the Mediterranean Libyan shore, closer to the border of Egypt. We were given a block of flats with some basic necessities and given jobs according to our qualifications.

I was employed in an agricultural project of figs, vine and almond trees. We had many Pakistani workers, the sea shore was sandy, and the blowing wind or strong breeze would take away all the sand around the small trees, and the workers kept shovelling back sand around the trees.

I did some grafting on almond trees. It was something interesting for a change. Once, when I was at the head office and needed a car to take me to the farm, I asked around for whom I should ask, and they sent me to the minister of agriculture of the Benghazi region. As I told him I needed a lift to the farm, he got up, came out of his room and shouted out the name of one of the drivers who came to give me a lift to the farm.

I found it interesting that a minster like him could do that. I liked that.

After a few months of working, I managed to accumulate some savings, as we did not have any expenses apart from food expenses. After about six months, the head of the UN sent me a message to go to see him, and booked a return flight ticket to Tripoli.

The return ticket cost me about fifty dinars, which was $150 to see the head of the UN, Aldo Sisignyano. He told me that he could get us an Italian tourist visa, provided that we could get another country's tourist visa.

I was sort of happy to do that, but when I told our group, no one accepted; even the friend who came with me when we left my country did not agree to come with me because I wanted to leave Libya.

But I decided to leave the country by myself. I managed to get a Poland tourist visa, and I told Aldo, 'I am going,' but the rest did not want to go.

I left by myself, as I thought living and working with Libyans was very difficult as it could cause me some trouble or even get me imprisoned. I didn't like the way they treated foreigners or us. A few whom I worked with were difficult and sometimes rude, but my manager, Mr Tahir Sanfaz, was nice and respectful. He kindly gave me a letter about my work experience in Libya.

I decided to leave. I did not know what would happen or where I would end up. I thought this was another risk I was taking, and I did leave.

My friend who was with me until then did not want to come and thought it was very risky. He came to the airport with me; on the way, he kept asking me, what guarantee did I have to be able to reach somewhere safe? I said, 'I know I am taking a risk, but I do not care, let it happen what it may'. It was not even guaranteed I could enter Italy.

I found out through experience one may have to take risks to make changes. Sometimes the changes required might be crucial to one's future and to have a good life. I learned that, in life, one cannot be scared of the obstacles, and stay shrivelled back, so bravery is needed at whatever cost to change one's life direction for the better and hopefully more prosperous life. And that's what I did.

One of those was my decision to leave, and I was happy to do so.

Leaving Libya

As I boarded the plane, the huge aeroplane was heavy with its passengers and loads. After a short while, squirming and granting to position itself to take off.

I felt as if it was like the plane was stuck on the hot grey tarmac, wanting to dislodge itself into the fresh air and take off.

I thought I had a similar feeling about my being there for about fifteen months, as it was so difficult to dislodge myself from the Libyan desert.

I felt I had something in common with this huge aeroplane.

It granted and dislodged itself and into the air, going up and above the Mediterranean sea, further up into the boundless light blue sky.

I was looking down from the window, little boats, ships scattered around in the blue sea, leaving lines of white froth behind, not thinking yet about how my arrival in Rome might be, and suddenly heard the captain say, 'Fasten your belt, get ready for landing'. It brought me back to where I was going, seeing the blue sea parted by a belt of pale sand and soon over the airport.

As we landed, I joined the queue and reached a bulky policeman sunk in his chair, without his head up, stamping all the green passports, including mine; then I found the colour of my passport was the same as the Libyans.

I got through with no problem. When I passed the control check, and there was nothing else, I found out I was in without a hitch, but my luggage had not arrived. I gave details about where I was going to stay and left. My friends were waiting at the gate.

I couldn't stay in Italy, as I had to go to the police station to sign a paper to leave Italy on the 31st of January, 1984, and fly to Poland, still counting days with worry and anxiety, not knowing what was next yet. I was with a friend for three nights and then got to know a few Kurdish students in L'Aquila, a mountainous town next to Gran Saso, the known high peak of Italy, about an hour and a half from Rome.

I didn't know any Italian. On the first day, I went into the town in the evening in the cobbled town square with many young people. I only understood 'Chau, Chau, Chau', which I had heard so many times.

Later, I thought, *yes, I might try to learn Italian. God knows how long I'm going to be here.*

I purchased a book on basic grammar and the way Italian letters read and pronounced and, with a Walkman and headphones, I started studying at home. I rented a room with a family that my friends helped me to find. I used to study every day by myself. After a few weeks, I went out to speak with my Kurdish students' Italian friends. It was often funny, but I didn't care.

When we got a telegram from the airport to pick up my luggage, my Kurdish friend gave me instructions on how to go to Rome and the airport with a few Italian words to get by. Whenever I remember this even now, it makes me laugh: I had to go by coach to Republic Square in Rome, and then try to find bus number three. I asked a bus driver where can I find 'Bus trre,' . He said, 'Not trie, trriee,' and he pronounced number 3 emphatically, as in my Kurdish language, 'trie' meant fart.

Later, I learnt from Kurdish students in Italy that I could get permission to stay in Italy through the UN office in Rome, or the UN could find another country for me to go to. I had the option to go to Canada through the Canadian Embassy. I was invited for an interview, but I ignored it. I didn't like to go as I thought it was too far and too cold, as we think the UK is like the next door to where I come from.

It took me three years to settle somewhere in the UK. I was in Bulgaria for two months, Libya for fifteen months, Italy for ten months, contacted UN office both in Tripoli and Roma we were a group of a few families, the rest of the group mostly went to Sweden, I ended up in the UK, and I love the UK

I arrived at UK Heathrow airport on the 6th of November, 1984. I was still not sure if they would let me stay, and they wanted me to go back the day after to Italy. That's where I should have been given asylum, but I refused and sought UK's UN legal assistance. It was called UKIS legal help, and after nine months stayed with exceptional leave to remain, and now, in 2022, it has been about thirty-six years since I have been in the UK.

I was not allowed to phone back home for about ten years, I was just an army deserter, and I had never been a politician. I tried hard to study the English Language, went back to University to improve my job prospects, and do interpreting and translation, and became a civil servant in Valuation Office Agency for over six years. I also did a few other jobs.

I deliberately wanted to have an English partner so I could improve my English; I think I did, as I have published about ten books in English and a few in Kurdish so far.

42

After the Chemical attack on Halabja in March 1988, when Saddam's regime used WMD, in the Guardian Newspaper I saw my uncle's house in Halabja with corpses of many lying in the street and on the pavement. I was desperate to know what had happened to my people, town, family, and neighbours. That's when I wrote a poem about the chemical attack on Halabja based on my brother's poem published in the Hawkary Kurdish newspaper in Iraq.

Halabja

When my heart is filled with desire and sadness
while my vision became blurred dull and rotten
Whenever I arrived in Halabja with a hearty anticipation,
I was inspired by the breeze of Mordana with the smell of its berries and
roses. It was my childhood's playground and like the cradle of our babies
Halabja was the sight of all my happiness and pride.
On 16th March 1988 my heart was broken, the gratitude of my
 hopeful youth
Was fiercely torn apart by Nerve Gas and taken, as the slaughter
 of our babies has filled my heart with pain and annihilation.
How shouldn't I run wildly and not complain for the shameful silence of
the believers in Human rights and their hypocrisy?

43

In 1991, when I was doing my English GCSE at Hammersmith West London College, I was often homesick, I wrote my second poem, it is a letter to a mountain called Surein. It was overlooking the agriculture project I managed until I left:

Dear Surein

Dear Surein I have a fear if I won't be able to see you again
To do like I used to do in early morning to come to Sharazur plain,
That lies before your feet so faithfully and obedient .
Refreshed my aspirations seeing your enormous existence,
your persistence. No war plane, no artillery,
And no advance technology
Would least bruise your resistance.

In 1992 our first baby boy was born. It was amazing for me, a father in exile. My love was next to me after ten years. He was like my nicest toy; I always played with him, made him walk when he was only seven and a half months, and he looked funny, a babe walking when I walked with him holding his hand.

I named him Surein. That is the name of the mountain I climbed when I left and crossed the border into exile.

As I often missed my family and friends, and the way of life back home. I tried to occupy my mind with reading, and I enrolled at university at West London Higher education, Brunel University, in 1992

I started doing sport, running for fitness. It was like I was trying to run away from homesickness and stress, and I took part in many half-marathons, and International marathons that gave me some pleasure, and I managed to raise some money for charity a few times.

I did twelve international marathons: eight in London, England; two in Tokyo, Japan; one in Stockholm, Sweden; one in Vilnius, Lithuania; and fourteen half-marathons in Hampshire, England.

I often tried to mix with people to socialise, but I was a bit too talkative; therefore, I tried to do various other things, like sport, reading, studying, and working.

I often went to the Kurdish Cultural centre in South East London to take part in sports and cultural activities. That was when I was contacted about taking part in creating an album comprised of pictures and poems, collaboration between poets and artists to produce an album for charity called, Strains of War, managed by a well-known lady called Amanda Sebastian.

I sent one of my poems, *Hands of Desperation*, about the Saddam regime's attack on civilian Kurds in South Kurdistan, North Iraq, in the March 1991

45

Uprising that ended up with over 30,000 civilian deaths. My poem was chosen and published in the London City Limits Magazine. It was the first time one of my poems was published in the UK:

Hands of Desperation

Many hands were stretched out
And have been raised only for bread.
Many hands were raised towards the sky,
To God, to cloud to rain, and snow,
Not to freeze to death, not to kill Kurdish children anymore.
The old in pain, the young in vain,
The babies were born in chilly wind under the rain.
They were hugged by the mountains, until their return or death.
But starving, freezing, dying and slaughter were much better than kneeling
down and surrender.

46

I often suffered from a bad night's sleep or insomnia for about ten years, from 1982, after I left my country. I could not get in touch with my family back home, as the law of the Iraqi regime deemed us traitors; if we had any communication, the regime would punish my family back home.

After ten years in exile and the 1991 Kurdish and Iraqi uprising the following year, in March 1992, I returned to Iraq and wrote the following:

Returning Back

After ten years, on the way back,
The plains, trees, and the mountains grey in the pale air,
As if worn out in distress from what they have witnessed.
The whole atmosphere was dead-silent; the water-
Streams were dried, and exposing:
Marble – skulls' grins of rocks, tree roots like bones,
Wielded together with clots of rusty mad-iron. Hardly any
Wild or domestic animals except a lonely little one, I
Guessed was trying disparately to find a companion, I
Found with her a few things in common.
I was looking into the far distance for any signs of life
Where could hardly see any
The shroud of snow was
Masking the reality of its existence

This was what is called the Iraq border area of Bashmakh.
Further on, there used to be a town of Penjwine, but oh
God, there's no more, it has been degraded almost to a
heap of rubble. No more villages can be seen; nothing
was popping up, would be standing for any sign of life.
The scarred bumpy roads with bombs, where used to be
shops, now are shacks with flimsy plastic roofs
mercilessly rattled by the gusty chilly wind.
The huddled shopkeepers behind their shacks' boxes,
with their sallow faces staring over a little log fires, into far
away distance, and trying to shrink in between their bony
shoulder blades, squatted on tin boxes and worn out
chairs. What was it now they were thinking of?
With hope for a better life, and would not be any more
strife.

Towards the Sharazur town, the plain:
There were slightly more familiar sceneries, as shades of
green going along the road and seeing a bit more
liveliness in a little bit milder atmosphere.
Further on, where it used to be the town of Sharazur,
where every standing building were brought down to
rubble, and were levelled with the rest of the plain.
The only signs of recognition were, the only little river, and
the two hilly peaks at each end. It was inconceivable and
so strange.
When I thought back of its past crowded liveliness, I
overcame with an intense emotion, pouring tears for what
has happened, I couldn't easily contain.
All these were bringing back memories of jostling crowds,
humble buildings,
schools, shops and bakeries into the past images' frame.
When I was comparing the two contrasting scenes I was
overwhelmed with endless grieve and pain. I was
contemplating, why, and how all that happened and who
is to blame?

A quarter mile outside the town:
Here are the village's skeletons: scars of headless pillars
stamped into the ground. A few lonely chameleons
standing before their dark holes, they were staring in
silence.
Thoughts ringing through my mind
From now back to my prime,
What has brought us face to face you the dirty parasite?
The toiling villagers in the fields from dawn to dusk, were
weeding, digging
and ploughing in the green fields. In mid-day heat, when
they were coming back for lunch covered in lush green up
to their knees.
Children used to play with colourful beads of gravel
splashing, and screaming with joy
in crystal streams.
In the shacks' shade the dark kettle
and the simmering tea. The cool water' clay pot with
dozing grandma in waiting to be waken up with chatting
farmers, and giggling kids.

48

The fresh bread, butter and cheese, the scarlet watermelon, slashed into two
and yogurt drink.to cool down the mid-summer heat.
Stretched and
lying down for a while a few was nodding to sleep.

Getting back to the car:
Gradually the Mercedes bus was plodding along
towards the city I left ten years before.
 It had spread out with no recognition
rippled with dark shades of rusty grey orange, and
gradually stretching long shadows at dusk.
Oh, it is already dark by the time I stepped out on the
familiar pavement, and the grey dusty tarmac.
The children were now adults, the adults were aged or
old, many were not there anymore soon I was cuddled,
hugged and whisked away to the comfort of my family. It
was so strange; who would think this is real I'm now
back?

49

One of the nights when I couldn't sleep until early morning I wrote the following:

Insomniac

I felt as if I was drowning in the dark ocean of night,
I was awake, and was staring at the stale pages of my fate.
I felt like, I was throwing my thoughts like disparate limbs,
To the sea shores' sharp ridges,
With anticipation to overcome: the droll, and the gloom of life.
My crammed chest was overwhelmed with distress
I was trying my best to make some room for happiness
If any left, therefore, I did not want to sleep, I did not resign to sea bed.

50

I often desired to translate classical Kurdish poetry into English, but it was difficult, as translating languages from different cultures is challenging. The following poem is from the Kurdish poet, Goran, who grew up and lived in Halabja in the 20th Century.

The Trip to the Hawraman

The chain of mountains high and defiant,
It's fully embracing the blue sky
The smooth white veil of the towering peaks
The solemn valleys and the dark woodland
The lingering trickles of the water streams,
are winding down in endless journeys.
The whining cries of the frothy currents
for lonely night, as comforting tunes.
Up and down in one's journey
Has a bitter tiredness, then a sweet relief.
Before arrival at the destined village
Into the orchard darted a slithering snake.

51

At the beginning of my exile life, I had to do any job available, labour, shop assistant, and sometimes cleaning jobs.

In the life of an exile, one has to restart their working life from scratch because back home, I was managing a sugar beet farm with many pieces of machinery and supervising about thirty workers.

In 1981, the first year of my farming job in the Sharazur plain, where I was managing the farm, I came first and the best in Iraq in regard to the quality and quantity of production, so my success was recognised, and I was rewarded for my hard work. That boosted my confidence to try to do my best ever since.

52

When I was at University in 1994, I managed the whole college user support by myself in the afternoons, and during the summer holidays, I was doing labour jobs in East London. One day, when I saw a young lady lying down on a patch of grass at a housing estate, sunbathing, I wrote a naughty poem for the first time. When I showed it to my boys' mother, she was surprised and said, 'You've never written anything like that!'

A Sun Bather

On her tummy a young blond was lying on the light green
lawn. Its blowing by the breeze, her silky nickers' yellow-orange.
The glaring midday heat was making pink-red her swelling
hips and thighs.

As a surreal dream, she was topless; I was tempted to
ask the time, anticipating raising her arms, seeing her firm
breast sending shivers through my spine. If the response
was not shut up, it would quicken my palpitation like the
church's bell of joy, would be stilled with astonishment
with her inviting smile before Venus coy.

After getting consent, I would roam my fingers on her
sweltering back for a while. Seeking her bosoms and
slipping in the tight gorge, contemplating no rescue, not to
come back to the fresh air of despair.

53

This is a poem I wrote about my attempts at trying to find a job.

Seeking employment

I'm getting ready, going for an interview:
I'm clean-shaven in my possible best
The name, address, and telephone number,
were all checked-up, and ready.
A glance at my watch quickened my pace,
No doubt there is another disappointment.
There was no alternative I gave it a chance.
Half an hour earlier, I was anxiously walking,
I was going up and down window shopping,
Until at last I rung and knocked, as if I was thrusting a
Heavy castle door, To meet a forged smile, hello.
Have a seat' he said I was given a board,
To fill in several pages with never ending blanks,
All were boring routines: experience, qualifications,
Skills, merits, and education.
Even the meeting was an obvious pretension,
As my details soon crammed the room: the name, ethnicity,
My oriental features, the worst was my accent.
Another actor shook my hand, lots of them
I have seen. With a false promise rattled my right arm again.
I wish I could dislodge that untruthfulness with his arm.

54

Summer 1994

We lived outside London, in the Guildford area with my family and children. I tried a lot with my wife, but I couldn't find a job, so I had to live in London. That was where I could manage to find a job, but because of the expense of commuting, I could not come home every day; instead, I always worked and stayed in London.

As we couldn't be together all the time, my relation with my family fell apart, and suddenly, I wasn't wanted back home anymore.

When that happened, my two sons were only 6 and 9 years. It was a disaster, as I adored my sons. I didn't think I would survive. My ex turned bitter. I told her, 'Go to your doctor to get help'. She didn't listen. My boys got distressed so much they contracted asthma for a while.

One evening, I went home for the weekend. She didn't allow me in when my boys ran toward me to cuddle me. Instead, she phoned the police! That was the most horrific evening of my life.

I felt worse than my childhood air raid, artillery bombing and shoot-out days. I was so desperate to be with my boys, so closed we were. She turned so bitter against me, she tried to convince them not to want me. Ever since then, I was 'stupid,' 'useless,' and all types of horrible expressions she could find. But she was so stupid she didn't understand my boys didn't like hearing bad things about me, their father.

When they were young, I acted like a child playing with them because I missed my childhood, as I had lost my mother and started working very early. I tried to revise my missed childhood, and I got back to enjoying my childhood again, often playing with them, taking them out, and buying anything I could for them; I loved to see them happy, singing for them to sleep in the evening.

The younger one retained a relationship with me. He often came to me whenever he could find time, but the older gradually didn't want to see me. He didn't communicate, didn't come out with me; whatever I did for him, he wouldn't react lovingly.

I was puzzled, stressed, and almost on the verge of crying. Why was his mother doing that? When I never touched her in a bad way and never used disrespectful language.

I was great when we were together, but when we separated, I was 'rubbish'.

I wrote the following about my younger boy, Zardusht, when he was always loving and wonderful:

To Zardi, Thank you

Thank you for being so loving and nice. Thank you for
your warm cuddle, little kisses, your little jokes and your
giggles.
Especially, at the weekend, when we often met for a few
hours, and then leave.
Thank you for being what you are, when you come up
With a joke,
A funny word that makes me smile or laugh.
Thank you for keeping me in the country if it wasn't for
You I would have left soon. Thank you for your beautiful
Looks, as my sisters says:
You are my exact copy, just like when I was little.
Thank you for being my dearest guest, when you come to
Me, you make the dead atmosphere of my flat so lively
And fresh, I always love to do for you my very best.
Thank you for caring for me, you do get worried when I'm
Upset.
When you are with me, you know, you are in place of all
my friends and family.
You know, when you leave me and go home, I get so
Upset for a while, my flat looks like an empty shell, I can
Do nothing when I realise we have made so much mess. I
Love seeing you are growing up tall and strong, but
Sometimes when we cross the road; I still try to hold your
Hand.
You sort of frown at me and withdraw your arm. Sorry my
Babe, my concern is for your safety. Oh, sorry again to
Call you a babe, but I shouldn't be
As you are, it is not a mistake. Even when you nudge me
With a vicious elbow, a funny frowning look and you say:
'I'm Zardi not your babe!' I hope you don't see this poem
As a credit card or a cheque, for buying silly expensive
Games, as you sometimes ask me and I refuse, it has

57

Been causing a little argument, I can't stand it as I see we
Both are angry or upset. But later, when we part we make
Up for it, with a cuddle, we say sorry and a kiss,
Sometimes it is so wonderful with
A nicely packaged M&S lobster to bring a smile back to
Your face...

The following is about my elder son Surein, who was my first love in exile. Anything he was made to do, never put me off him. This was about how much I was missing him.

Please come to me

Please come to me I am nearby; you keep away from me
I never know why?
Please come to me I am not away, I love to hear whatever
You say
I am here alone, I don't know how long. I just want to
Know how you getting on. Please come to me yes you
Are my son, come truly tell me what wrong I have done.
Whatever happened, they are in the past, I never meant
It, shouldn't make you sad. You should trust me, never tell
You lies I never do that upon my own life.

The following poem is about how I was upset sometime:

I just can't believe it

You turned away from me just like I was a stranger.
For many years I have been alone. I thought you were
the first to give me a smile of hope, so much I was longing for.
I am now so puzzled I don't know what to do, and how to cope.
I have had no one for so long; I thought you were the first to be truly mine.
Now, you turned away from me, just like I'm a stranger.
Was I wrong to hate leaving you, when you were young?
Was I wrong to feel so great holding your hand?
Was I wrong thinking about you would make me smile, giving me so much pleasure that glowed my heart?
Oh, I wish I could read your mind, to get the answer I need, to give me peace.
For once, I felt I wasn't alone anymore; you gave me smile I was so much longing for. Is life really so cruel? To use one of my most loved one against his dad, for anyone who does would be so fool.
Still, I cannot believe that, as you are my own flesh and blood.
I have never thought, you would consciously ever do that.
If you don't give me the answer, I will tell you the truth. I may simply go mad.
Whatever you do and think of me, I will still love you so much, whatever age you may be, you are always my babe and I am always your Dad.

I came to the UK seeking asylum and peace. That was the type of peace I was getting. I left twenty-one of my marathon medals with my son, but I later found out my ex threw all of them away. But my son Surein did make me proud for becoming one of the best mathematicians in the world when in 2009, he won the Cambridge University Young Scientist of the year when he took part in an International competition, he wrote *Beauty in Mathematics*, by Surein Aziz. It's on google.

My sons, Surein and Zardi are my love of life. We are now fine, I love life because of them.

…

I tried to improve my job prospects; I did a modular degree in business management and art, just like I had dreamed during my childhood of exploring the mountains around Halabja. I started exploring new cultures, learning many good habits: sports, poetry, novels and writing; I wrote an essay called: 'Aspects of primitive and spiritual in Abstract Art'. It was about the philosophy of Abstract Art. I just loved doing that. It turned out to be very good, and I just published it in February 2022

I started publishing many articles on a Kurdish website about politics, poetry and history, etc., in Kurdish and in English.

I was doing many things at the same time: reading books, doing sports, studying and attending university, working and enjoying my precious leisure time when I was with my sons. I guess it was a kind of escapism from being homesick, of being away from my boys when we separated, and from the rest of the family back home, and avoiding distressing news about the war situation back home.

61

Once I saw a picture of a six-year-old girl in The Guardian Newspaper
from South East Turkey, North Kurdistan, with an article about persecution
of non-Turks there, especially Kurds.

The image was so powerful I wrote a poem about a picture of a torn-apart
Kurdish toddler. It was published in the student Union magazine, West
London College of Higher Education.

In Kurdistan

In South East Turkey Kurdistan, a NATO tank is out of hand.
It was chasing a six year old girl; she was glancing with goggled eyes
And screaming on scorched bare feet, assumed a PKK terrorist. She was
heading to the rugged mountains, under the darkened horizon of her
detonated village.
No going back but to fight, or to divert a bomb a bullet
from her uncles' chest, the true icon of struggle, resilience and human
right.

62

At the time my political views were different, but now, I never condone violence.

The following is an old Kurdish song by Hasan Zirak, a well-known and great Kurdish artist, I often used to hear it in my childhood, and teenage years, it's a romantic song I translated to English, In Kurdish is called *hey nar hey nar*.

Hey Fire, Hey Fire

Hey fire; hey fire with the cool summer breeze was so much desire
For meeting again as if on fire, as the cool water spring wouldn't quench my thirst and no sleeping pill can put me at rest.
In the late summer evening are melodies and tunes
That comes from a far from the memories and dreams, of the playfulness of the uncaring time, that passed so fast and always thought you were mine that can't be brought back the glows of our happiness,
Hey fire, hey fire my heart has no rest
Hey fire Hey fire that has brought back so much longing and desire, as the memory of meeting puts me on fire that lifts my longing with insatiable desire, in the colourful orchards, the singing birds
With roses, flowers, fresh green leaves, and buds, in the cool summer shades
For the last gasping and rest, as for our playfulness we had so many quests.
Hey fire, hey fire, I have so much desire, for the past memories, my heart is on fire

63

In 2011, I took part in a jury Service in London as an Indian young man
had murdered his mate after his friend had got hold of his Barclays Bank card
and lost all his savings to online gambling:

It was Strange

It was late evening when I was at 71 Bannockburn Road
It was getting dark; no one was around, so strange
I looked around; upstairs faint light was on,
Downstairs' darkness was locked up in silence
Checked the one after next door, there was the Indian temple.
The CCTV camera was still looking on;
I glanced at the passing by Brook-din Road from the right.
I walked down from its left a few doors... more doors until
It was 87.
I walked back to 71, paused with reflection.
What brought me here? I thought. I had a sad and strange
connection.
The house is still here, the shapes are not much different;
I remembered others who left on Friday, the 7th of January, 2011.
For whatever reason
They've never come back, each of them for a different
reason: one of them in Belmarsh Prison, the other is not
with us anymore not with a very good excuse.
That was never required by any wisdom or reason, it was senseless.
Their departure created so many other connections: a few people, different
Routes of travel, words like Jury, Usher, court gallery, deliberation,
People, friends we never thought of meeting.
Memories events, so many scars left.
As I remembered all that I was so upset,
Whoever lives there now, as if life has been routine.
For the new lodgers, it is better not to know,

As the scars left none of us wished to experience how, what for, or why all that happened?

And after the Jury verdict was murder, I wrote the following:

As long as we live
As long as we live, we think or believe
One day we will walk like a millionaire.
No more we would care, we will be relieved.
Nowhere will be far noting will be dear.
As long as we live, we tend to believe
One day we will walk like a millionaire.
Just think of the dream, you know what I mean.
May never come true, it's only a wish, one may think it is
due.
As long as we live, we tend to believe one day
We will walk as a millionaire. We will never know, it is not
out of reach
We have to believe one day will be there.
That is how we should live, one has to believe.
How anyone can cope to live without hope?
We all have our dreams, that is true it seems
One day we will walk just like a millionaire.

With my family went to the Isle of White for a short holiday. On the first day, we walked around and up to the Shancklin height overlooking the sea. As I saw the spectacle, I wrote the following:

Shancklin

I am standing high on the
Shancklin cliff, in the shimmering air I breathe.
It is mystic, romantic and
The boundless space has put me at ease.
I was stepping forward with a temptation of looking
Further beneath, the fence did away with
my fear not to go any further boosting my excuse.
Bracing the crinkled Carpet of the blue sea
That was haunted by solemn clouds, as if soon bursting in to tears.

I heard on the news there had been a strong earthquake in North Kurdistan, South East Turkey, with many casualties. It had occurred about the time of the Muslim religious feat Eid Al Adha, the Eid of Sacrifice. It inspired me to write the following:

There is no Eid

Let's not celebrate; there is no Eid because of the ruthless crimes of
the fascists. As in the town of Van, in South East Turkey
Many became victims of an earthquake.
For the cruel stand of Erdogan, the fascist Turkish government,
In the first 24 hours didn't let in any outside assistance.
They left all the families for dead, crashed, trapped under their buildings
For them, there is no Eid
Look! What happened brother Muslims?
How can anyone celebrate Eid of forgiveness and sacrifice?
To see so many children killed, orphans injured or hardly survived,
No parents, no sisters, no brothers, have nowhere to go.
How can it be right to freeze in the chilling merciless wind?
No food, no shelter, there is no Eid celebration
It is senseless, there is no Eid! Where are friends, where are families?
What happened to our brother Muslims who don't give a toss?
The buzzing towns and villages are now silent turned to rubble
All were turned to a cemetery.
Where are observers of human right?
Where are proctors of human pride? We can now clearly see.

67

They are all a bunch of liars who are silent, who are blind, who can't see the truth; no way their silence can be justified.

It was after my niece's death from breast cancer, I was very upset and in the evenings, I often walked to the park and a pond near where I lived in South East London to get some fresh air and enjoy the beauty of nature at sunset. I wrote the following:

It is the Late Evening

It's the late evening, the end of the day
Whatever we do, whatever we say, we hope tomorrow
Things will be fine, we should not bother whether yours or mine,
As there is another day.
The day that has past, whether good or bad, that was destiny.
We shouldn't be sad, as there is another day.
We hope tomorrow will be a good day let's hope that way
For a nicer one, that's what we should say.
We should try our best however we can and hope it will be okay.
It is the late evening the end of the day, whatever we think whatever we say,
We hope tomorrow will say that is the one; we try our best however we can.
That is how we should think, why should we worry if there is another day?
For the days that past, whether good or bad, we see we've survived.
As there is another day, that followed the last, hope for the brightest day.
That is how we can survive, and try for another one as much as we can, we should always say, and hope for the following day, this should be the way, and hope will be okay.

I had a contact online from Ukraine, often talked, and she spoke little English. The following is one of our chat:

On the Chat line we met
She said, 'I don't know English'. I said, 'don't worry, your English is fine'.
She said, 'I have got cold'. I said, 'How is your throat?'
She said, 'I am taking antibiotics, sorry, I don't understand'.
I said, 'Throat is the tube between your mouth and your chest'
Chest is the box between your neck and stomach'.
She said, 'Yes'.
I said, 'Lips, that is what I hope to kiss'.
She said, 'Ha ha ha, now I understand'.
And I said, 'The heart is where my love is'.
She said, 'I remember you are an artist'.
I said, 'You see I can write a poem or lyrics'.
She said, 'I will write the music'.
I said, 'These are all true, coz your beauty is so sublime'
So, I have to copy it, as we try our dreams to come true'.
She said, 'That would be nice.'
I said, 'I know darling that would be so sweet to meet.'

In 2005, a group of friends and I who often got together to write and share our approach and understanding of poetry and literature published a small book. The following is one of the poems about the Gulan cemetery:

Mulberry Tree

Late spring afternoon heat
In Gulan, Halabja under clumps of trees
The smashed, stamped mulberries
Smell sweet in the shade.
They attract crowds of sparrows, chicks
Hornets and bees
Up there it is heaving with life and noise
Unlike the congregation
Further beneath.

71

For my niece, who was thirty-three when she died from breast cancer in London in 2005.

To Kani

Oh, thinking of you, you are not here anymore, so many unanswered questions.
No one knows: why, what for and
Who is to blame? You were taken away so soon
When your youth has seen nothing
Like its full-moon. You were only eight months when your father gone
It is strange, these things happen unexpected and so sudden.
I am still thinking why life for some is just like that.
Why life for someone like you has gone so wrong, it is mad
When you were told just a few days left,
'It is not fair', you said. Yes, it was unfair, but who is to blame
Who doesn't bother or care? One always wonders:
Who decides for us to come and leave in whatever way?
Whoever's will, it is not right to switch off, to close
the window of life mercilessly so tight. Oh, it is damn wrong to think about it and decide.
Isn't it a false happiness? When we come and go
when it may end like that. With so many broken hearts
It is unbelievably hard. When I think back or look far ahead
What is the point, however it may last. We eventually end up dead, sad, mad, however it may end, and it is so bad. It is so strange neither our coming nor our going is in our hands. However our days, weeks years pass, we have not got a clue however they may last.

The following is about the European Union:

The EU

A Pig in a suit or a wolf in ship's skin
crisp white collars raised their chins,
like proud snouts. Rounding a stable
each with a knob for exacerbating talks.
In their pockets or their brains Hagel's, Kant's and Plato's philosophy
Maastricht treaty and ERM each country's presidency is for a sixth month
For the trade pact leave their borders wide, but in the face of immigration
They close it to insulate their national pride.

I used to work for Valuation Office, Inland Revenue, in London.

When I got closer than I should have to a friend,

 I wrote the following:

To my Friend

Last night, I met someone very nice on the coach, but not
as much as you. Can there ever be space in one heart for
two? You may still ignore me as you always do. I will have
to wait and see, to go up and down. Try an excuse to
come around. Until at last, either you shoot my head, drop
me dead, or into your heart let me through. 'If I'm not
already there',
If you think I have offended you and are being cheeky, I sincerely plead
for amnesty.

When in 1996 I graduated, and left at the College of Higher education,
Isle worth London UK, I wrote the following about a friend:

Leaving College

You left, I was left with emptiness:
Your words were cold; your eyes on the hollow horizon were still.
No gaze, no talk, no more of exuberant jokes,
You left me with a painful Silence.
I said a dreadful good bye with no hidden expression,
No need to say why, you left me with a painful silence.

75

I first published in the Kurdistan Tribune in 2013 written

By Kazhal Ebrahim Khidre. Translated and introduced by Yasin Aziz:
'Two years ago, in March, I was in Halabja and I came across this poem in
Klil Kurdish Magazine. I found it so powerful. It seems to tell the whole
story of what happened to South Kurdistan in our recent history.

'I don't know this poet, but I felt I shared what she says. When I read it the
first time, it made me shiver…

For tens of times

I went back to the season of loneliness. I am the heart of a left out orchard
full of tears, a graveyard with no birds, no glowing moon. I have met a girl
with no name or address.
Many times I have passed through the dark autumn of romance
So often they came across their own death in the mad ocean of waves.
I am not a trespasser into an orchard full of flowers of life
I have come from the spring of blood, I feel like I am in the left out boat
After calmed down waves of a raged sea, it is now serene…
The greyness of my hair is like glitters of the water stream,
My instinct is like a dropped leaf. I have come holding no pass,
from a hell into the flames of another.
From the edge of a plain that was ornamented with flowers
of wounds, mixed with dark shades of a broken-hearted butterfly.
I was born and came. I have not come just by chance, I came in
the freezing winter with torrential rain, From a collapsed town, derelict
and abandoned, that was where I was born.
In order to wear the mourning black dress as my father left.
A poem came in black like a dress to enclose me, I cried like a bird
A breeze of music, a foreigner narrated to me. I have not come just by
myself to be in the world of broken-heartedness with pain,
the burnt out corpse of a woman, from Halabja. That became like ash coal
of anger that made me rewrite their inflictions.

I have not come to be a caught up prisoner, I heard cries of poor children of Kirkuk that made me get into the world of struggle like little beautiful girls of Qandil.
If one day, I happened to disappear from my town, you may ask the cherry trees of the Seiwan Cemetery,
That's where the autumn leaves scattered and fallen, I might be visiting a martyr's grave, if you can't find me, I might be in
The collapsed alleys of Qlladiza town, at the house of Pakiza, who
was the victim of the Garmyian Anfal/Auschwitz campaign.
If you still couldn't find me, I might have become a white pigeon
Or a bird to sing for the tall figure of this nation, or I might have become
A tender poem for a headstone of the graveyard,
like a dropped bud of a dear wrinkled flower…

I wrote the following when I heard a young Kurdish girl from Syria took her own life when run out of ammunition not to be a slave in the hands of IS:

To Jailan,

You are the beacon of hope and the flower of struggle:
The one, who never wanted to be enslaved,.
I know how you felt, when you took your own life; not to be
amongst the criminals' concubines. Those who
Are bartered with in the hands of the IS gang's thugs, the
ones who would bring back Stone Age's ethos of
plunder and genocide.

I can imagine when you decided your own fate, as
For Kurds, it is the fact of life nowhere remains
Safe; when we turn back, our history is stale
With stories of Halabja, Garmian and Bahdinan Anfal genocide campaigns
The track record shows, we hardly have true friends…

I wrote the following when I heard on the news Nelson Mandela had died:

When I heard Mandela died

The symbol of freedom, the light of Hope
has really subsided? When I heard Nelson Mandela died
for his enormous soul I uncontrollably cried
That carried on and defied 27 years in prison.
He came out with no blemish, to start afresh and he sought no rest,
to finish off the mission was not a surprise.
Mandela was a symbol like a huge monument that towered the world against fascism.
Mandela's mission like a banner of hope to all mankind is always there for equality and freedom.

Author

My two fantastic boys, when they were young.

A few medals of my Marathons, published in Inland Revenue Valuation Office magazine in 2000

82

Afterword

I think I could have put some highlights of my life through poetry in this book, as I have a lot more. I hope I can put it in another book. As for some of them, I would like to call them prose, not poetry.

I think I have managed to overcome all or most adversity in life, but I don't think I can ever overcome the loss of my mother.

I do yet feel, despite all the near-death dangers I have experienced, I have done well. My message for anyone is to believe in yourself and never give up hope.

Thank you for reading my book.

My Instagram, Kurdo7492 for my artworks and some more poetry.

Halabja Town